SALMON

Tom Jackson

Grolier
an imprint of

SCHOLASTIC

www.scholastic.com/librarypublishing

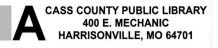

Published 2008 by Grolier
An imprint of Scholastic Library Publishing
Old Sherman Turnpike, Danbury,
Connecticut 06816

For The Brown Reference Group plc
Project Editor: Jolyon Goddard
Copy-editors: Ann Baggaley, Tom Jackson
Picture Researcher: Clare Newman
Designers: Jeni Child, Lynne Ross,
    Sarah Williams
Managing Editor: Bridget Giles

Volume ISBN-13: 978-0-7172-6284-7
Volume ISBN-10: 0-7172-6284-7

**Library of Congress
Cataloging-in-Publication Data**

Nature's children. Set 3.
    p. cm.
    Includes bibliographical references and
index.
    ISBN 13: 978-0-7172-8082-7
    ISBN 10: 0-7172-8082-9
    1. Animals--Encyclopedias, Juvenile. I.
    Grolier Educational (Firm)
    QL49.N384 2008
    590.3--dc22

                        2007031568

Printed and bound in China

PICTURE CREDITS

Front Cover: **Alamy:** Steve Bloom Images.

Back Cover: **Nature PL:** Brandon Cole,
Michel Roggo; **Photolibrary.com:** Richard
Hermann, Bernd Rommelt.

Ardea: Jason Mason 13; **Corbis:** Natalie
Fober 17, 23; **Nature PL:** Michel Roggo 10,
21, 26–27, 42, Peter Scoones 38, 45, Lynn M.
Stone 46, Kim Taylor 5, 22; **NHPA:** George
Bernard 9, Lutra 14; **Photolibrary.com:**
Joyce and Frank Burek 4, 29; **Shutterstock:**
David Brimm 41, Michael J. Thompson 34;
Still Pictures: Kelvin Aitken 33, Klaus Jost 6,
J. Mallwitz/Wildlife 18, Schafer and Hill 2–3, 30.

Contents

FACT FILE: Salmon

Class	Ray-finned fish (Actinopterygii)
Order	Salmon-shaped fish (Salmoniformes)
Family	Salmon (Salmonidae)
Genera	Atlantic salmon (*Salmo*) and Pacific salmon (*Oncorhynchus*)
Species	Atlantic salmon and six species of Pacific salmon—cherry salmon, chinook salmon, chum salmon, coho salmon, pink salmon, and sockeye salmon
World distribution	Most live in the North Pacific and North Atlantic Oceans and the rivers around them; cherry salmon live in the western Pacific
Habitat	Born in freshwater, the salmon then travel to the salty ocean to grow; they then swim back up rivers to breed before dying
Distinctive physical characteristics	All have pink flesh; although they range in size from 2 to 120 pounds (1–55 kg)
Habits	Migrate long distances from the sea to freshwater rivers and streams for spawning
Diet	Krill and shrimp

Introduction

Salmon are a mystery to **biologists**. They begin life in rivers and streams, far inland. As they grow up, the salmon swim to the sea. Adult salmon spend years in the deep ocean, before they swim back into rivers to have babies of their own. Each salmon returns to the exact same river in which it was born. But how does the fish know which river to swim up? Biologists have spend many years trying to answer that question. They now have several clues as to the answer, but it still remains one of the great mysteries of the natural world.

Salmon are powerful swimmers. They can swim against very strong currents.

5

Pink salmon eggs are soft. They do not have hard shells like birds' or reptiles' eggs.

Buried Treasure

Salmon lay pea-sized eggs in clear streams with a strong current. To make sure the little eggs do not get washed away by the water, the mother salmon buries them under gravel and sand at the bottom of the stream. There, the eggs are safe and hidden from hungry **predators**. Although buried, clean water still manages to flow around the eggs, keeping them healthy.

It takes all winter for the baby salmon to grow inside the eggs. The streambed contains many thousands of them. All of them will hatch at about the same time, filling the stream with tiny fish. When the young hatch, their parents will not be around to protect their offspring from predators or to help them grow.

See-through Baby

After a couple of weeks, two tiny specks of black
show up inside the egg. They are the eyes
of the baby inside. The baby has a lot more
growing to do before it is time to leave its egg.
Salmon usually hatch in late winter or early
spring, when the rivers are full of water from
rain and melted snow.

The tiny fish struggle free of the gel-like egg.
This stage in a salmon's life is known as the
alevin (AH-LUH-VIN). An alevin does not eat.
Instead it lives off yolk taken from inside the
egg. Yolk is full of the nutrients the young fish
needs. The alevin carries the yellow yolk with it
in a sac under its body.

The scales of an alevin are so thin that its body is almost see-through.

As an alevin grows
larger, its scales
become darker
and thicker.

Small Fry

At first, the alevin stays hidden in the gravel, surviving on its supply of yolk. After four to six weeks, depending on water temperature, it is usually strong enough to fight against the stream's current. The alevin wriggles out of hiding and starts to swim in the water. As the alevin grows stronger, the yolk sac shrinks. By the time the yolk is completely gone, the alevin has grown into a more fishlike shape. It is now a **fry**, or parr.

Salmon fry are less than an inch (2.5 cm) long, but they already look like adult fish. They have scales all over their body. Also, the few large frilly **fins** that they had when they were alevin have divided up. The fry now have the same number and arrangement of fins as they will have as adult salmon.

A First Meal

The salmon fry are now old enough to eat food. At first they swim with their mouth open to catch any bit of food that drifts by. But soon the fry learn how to find the food they want. They start off by hunting insect **larvae**—the young forms of insects. At first the fry go for larvae that have just hatched from their egg. Later on, when they have grown some more, the fry can tackle larger larvae, such as the nymphs of dragonflies.

Most adult insects do not live underwater. However, the fry also learn to grab any adult insects that are walking on the water's surface or have fallen in from overhanging branches.

While hunting for insects, the fry must also be aware of any predators that might be hunting them. Larger fish, such as trout, eels, and perch, eat a lot of salmon fry. The young salmon are also caught by kingfishers and otters.

Salmon fry swim
in groups, or
shoals, for safety.

A smolt looks like a small version of an adult salmon.

Life Changing

Salmon fry live in the streams and rivers close to where they were born until they are two or three years old. At about this time, their body starts to change once again. These changes prepare the young fish for adult life in the ocean. During this "teenage" stage—halfway between being a child and an adult—the salmon is known as a **smolt**.

Once the salmon become smolts, they begin the long journey to the ocean. They set off downstream, swimming from the small streams into the larger rivers. Smolts all over the area begin the journey around the same time. Soon there are many thousands of smolts crowded into the main rivers. Their journey to the sea is a long one. Some smolts travel 1,800 miles (3,000 km).

At the Ocean

Eventually the smolts reach the mouth of the river, where the water from the sea mixes with the river. Seawater is full of salt, while the river carries **freshwater**. Most fish can survive only in one type of water. Cod and tuna are saltwater fish. They would die if they swam into a river. On the other hand, carp, like pet goldfish, can live only in freshwater.

However, salmon are special fish. They can move from freshwater to saltwater—and then back again—without too much trouble. The smolts take a break from their journey when they reach the sea. They stay near the coast to get used to the taste of the water—they will need to recognize the flavor later in their life. Finally, the young salmon head out to sea.

Salmon smolts gather in large shoals when they reach the mouth of the river.

A salmon spends about half of its life in freshwater and half in the sea.

Tastes Salty!

Seawater tastes really salty, and it is not fun to swallow. If you swallowed seawater, it would actually make you more thirsty. Your body would have to use a lot of the water already inside it to wash all the sea salt away. Once it has done that, there will be less water left in your body than before, so you need another drink—of freshwater this time.

Fish have similar problems with salt. Those that live in freshwater have more salt inside their body than in the surrounding water. That causes water from the outside to be drawn into their body through their skin. Freshwater fish, therefore, have special ways of removing the extra water they absorb, or they would pop. Saltwater fish have less salt inside their body than in the surrounding water. That results in water being constantly drawn out from their body. Saltwater fish must, therefore, drink a lot to replace this lost water or they would dry out. Salmon, unlike most fish, can do all of these things and can live in almost any kind of water.

Fish Family

Salmon belong to a family of fish called the Salmonidae. That is a large group that also includes trout, graylings, and bloaters. Some of the family members, such as some of the trout, make a journey similar to the one that salmon make. They swim from the sea back up the rivers to breed. However, trout do not return to the exact same place as where they hatched, as salmon do. The trout are happy to breed in the same general area as where they were born.

There are seven species of salmon in all. One species is the Atlantic salmon. The other six species are Pacific salmon. Salmon all live in northern parts of the oceans. That is because they prefer cold water. Salmon like water that is colder than a chilly 57°F (14°C). Most human swimmers would find water temperatures that low very uncomfortable.

Rainbow trout do not head out to sea, but spend their whole life in rivers and lakes.

An adult male Atlantic salmon leaps up a waterfall in Scotland.

Atlantic Salmon

Atlantic salmon start their life in the rivers and streams of eastern North America and northwestern Europe. As their name suggests, when Atlantic salmon are old enough they swim out into the Atlantic Ocean.

Atlantic salmon have been caught by people for hundreds of years, especially in places such as Scandinavia and Scotland. Like all salmon, the Atlantic have tasty, pink colored flesh. When the flesh is smoked, it turns a dark orange.

There is a funny Scottish legend about how the first salmon got smoked. Two neighbors were arguing and in his frustration one decided to throw fish at the other. One fish, a large salmon caught from the river, fell into the chimney of the neighbor's house. It got stuck and over the next few weeks, the fish was smoked by the wood burning in the fireplace beneath. When the fish was found, its flesh tasted delicious—and Scottish people have been smoking salmon ever since.

Pacific Salmon

Six out of the seven total salmon species live in the north Pacific region. Five of these Pacific species—the chinook, the chum, the coho, the pink and the sockeye, or blueback, salmon—are found in the waters off North America. These five species mainly lay their eggs in the rivers of Alaska, British Colombia, and the western United States. However, some members of all five species swim into the rivers of Siberia, China, Korea, and Japan to lay their eggs.

One Pacific species, the cherry salmon, is restricted to the waters around Japan. It always heads to that region to lay its eggs.

Some Pacific salmon have been introduced to new places. For example, people have transported eggs and alevin to rivers in Chile. Today several types of salmon live in these rivers and the waters of the southern Pacific Ocean.

All Grown Up

An adult salmon is built for swimming quickly. It has a long, streamlined body that allows it to easily slice through the water. Its body is covered in many rows of shiny, tough scales. These scales protect the salmon from being injured, but also stop it from losing water too quickly—now that it is out to sea. The scales are covered in a slippery slime, called mucus. This mucus makes the skin waterproof and also helps fight off any harmful germs that might be in the water.

A salmon is powered forward by its V-shaped tail waving from side to side. The tail also does most of the steering. The four small fins on the belly are used for fine-tuning the position of the salmon's body. The two larger fins, one under the tail, the other on the back, act like a keel. They stop the fish from rolling sideways.

Sockeye salmon develop bright red scales when they are ready to breed.

Camouflaged Fish

Adult salmon are not all the same size. Some are fully grown when they reach 2⅕ pounds (1 kg). Others continue growing for longer and can achieve weights of as much as 120 pounds (55 kg). These giant salmon stay out at sea a lot longer than their smaller relatives and might never return to a river to breed. A normal size for a salmon is around 29 pounds (13 kg).

Most salmon have dark spots on their back and a silvery colored belly. This color pattern keeps the salmon hidden in the water. Looking at a salmon out of water, it is difficult to see how the pattern helps. However, underwater the conditions are very different. The dark spots camouflage the fish when looking from above. The pattern blends in with the water ripples and rocky bottom. A predator swimming below the salmon would also find it hard to spot. The silvery belly is the same color as the bright surface of the water.

The chinook
salmon is among
the largest of the
Pacific species.

Salmon pump water over their gills by opening and closing their mouths.

Breathing Water

Animals need oxygen to survive. Humans process the oxygen they breathe in from the air in their lungs. However, salmon do not have lungs and they cannot breathe air. So how do salmon get the oxygen they need to survive?

Water has oxygen mixed into it. Salmon, and most other fish, use **gills** to take the oxygen out of the water. A fish has two gills, one positioned on each side of the head. The gills are inside the head underneath large, round flaps of skin called gill covers. The gills are bright red because they are full of blood.

A fish breathes by sucking water into its mouth. The water washes over the gills, and then out of the slits behind the gill covers. As the water moves past, the oxygen in it is picked up by a special substance in the blood inside the gills. The blood then carries the oxygen it has picked up around the body.

Pink Food

Salmon and their relatives, trout, are known for their pink-colored flesh. Before salmon reach the ocean, their flesh is white and gray, like that of most other types of fish. It only turns pink after the salmon start to live and feed in the sea.

A salmon's main foods are shrimp and smaller relatives of shrimp called **krill**. Shrimp and krill live in huge shoals that are washed along by ocean currents. Salmon twist and turn inside the shoal, eating their **prey** in huge amounts. Shrimp and krill are pink. It is this food that makes the salmon pink themselves. Salmon also eat smaller fish, such as smelt and herring, and squid.

Krill, tiny relatives of lobsters and crabs, are a favorite food of salmon.

A grizzly bear eats a salmon caught from a waterfall in Alaska.

Salmon Hunters

Salmon are hunting fish, but they are also hunted themselves. Human anglers collect large numbers of smolts with nets and they also catch adult salmon as they return to rivers to **spawn**. Another big threat is the brown bears, such as grizzlies, that gather in river pools to scoop salmon out of the water.

Unfortunately, when they are out at sea, salmon have even more enemies. Sharp-eyed hunting birds, such as sea eagles, herring gulls, and comorants, pick off any salmon that swim too close to the surface.

Enemies lurk in deeper water as well. Salmon are a favorite food of sea lions, porpoises, and even orcas, or killer whales. Sharks and large fish, such as cod and tuna, also prey on salmon.

Following Its Nose

Salmon spend three or four years at sea. It is then time to head back to the rivers of their birth. Amazingly, the fish do not get lost. No matter how far they have wandered out to sea, when the time comes, the salmon instinctively return to their birth river. How do they do it?

The answer is still a bit of a mystery. Biologists believe the salmon use a built-in compass to find the correct coast. The fish then use their powerful sense of smell to sniff out the river from which they first entered the sea. Each river has its own particular odor. The smell comes from the different things that get mixed into the river's water. These are the remains of plants and soil from along the river's banks, and the minerals washed out of rocks.

Sockeye salmon travel for many weeks to reach the rivers along the West Coast of North America.

Pink salmon are also called humpbacked salmon, because the males develop a ridge behind the head when they are ready to breed.

Growing Apart

As they head for their home river in spring, salmon change one last time. The females have thousands of pink eggs growing inside them. As a result, the females develop bulges on both sides of their body.

The males do not grow plump. In fact, they become thinner and develop a fierce look. Their eyes sink into their head, and the lower jaw grows longer than the upper one. The male salmon now have a jutting jaw armed with pointed teeth. These changes make the male salmon into fighting machines. When the time comes, they will have to fight one another for the females.

Swimming Upstream

Once the returning salmon enter their birth river, they stop eating. Most species will never eat again. The journey upstream is a one-way trip. The salmon rely on fat stored inside their body to power them up the stream. And they need all the power they can get as they swim against the current.

The salmon are strong enough to force their way up rapids and to jump over waterfalls. They often gather in groups at the bottom of these obstacles, taking a rest before starting the climb.

Many of the salmon's rivers have been dammed. The huge dams generate electricity and make it easier for boats to travel up and down the river. However, they also block the path for returning salmon. Even salmon cannot leap over a giant dam. Dam builders construct salmon ladders for them instead. These are concrete pools arranged like flights of steps. The salmon can climb these ladders just like a series of waterfalls, to get up and over the dam.

Salmon jump between pools using a salmon ladder on the Feather River in California.

A female sockeye
salmon digs a redd
in the bed of the
Adam's River in
southern Canada.

A Homecoming

Eventually the salmon arrive in the shallow streams where they were born a few years before. They may find themselves with brothers and sisters they last saw as fry.

After the long journey, the salmon rest in the shady water. They are tired, but their work is not yet over. The female salmon begin to search the river bottom for areas of gravel that would make a suitable site for a nest of eggs, known as a **redd**. The strongest females chase weaker fish away from the best sites.

Once a female has taken control of a site, she begins to dig her redd. She does this by rolling on to her side and fluttering her tail to push gravel out of the way. Digging the redd takes time. She might dig down as far as 1.5 feet (0.5 m). The female will have to take several rests before she has finished building the redd.

Waiting Game

Once a female salmon has completed her redd, she will lay some of her eggs in it. Each redd contains a few hundred eggs. While she is still digging, males gather around her. They all want to be the first in the line when she lays some eggs. The largest male chases the smaller ones away. Once the eggs are laid, the male darts into the redd and releases **sperm** over them. Each egg needs to be **fertilized** by a sperm before it can grow into a new fish. Other males jostle in to deliver some sperm of their own. If they are lucky it might fertilize one or two of the eggs.

The males then swim off to look for another female that has yet to lay her eggs. After laying her first batch of eggs, the female then moves upstream and begins to dig another hollow to make a redd. The gravel from that redd will cover the first hole, securing the precious eggs.

Two large, male
pink salmon wait
behind a female
as she prepares
her redd.

The body of a female sockeye salmon is washed up after it has finished breeding.

Tired to Death

Salmon spawn, or breed, all summer. A female salmon may dig several redds in all, until her eggs finally run out as fall approaches. The males dart to and fro, fighting for the chance to fertilize as many eggs as possible. Once spawning is over, the salmon are exhausted. A few Atlantic salmon have enough strength to swim back to the sea. They then feed and rest before coming back to spawn a second time. However, most Atlantic salmon and all Pacific salmon are too tired to reach the sea. They slowly swim downstream. Their fins are in tatters from the fighting and digging. They begin to die one by one. In some rivers, their bodies fill the water.

Recycled Bodies

The sight of many hundreds of dead fish might seem sad, but it is completely natural. In fact, the dying fish are giving their offspring just what they need to get a good start in life. The fish's bodies decay and provide food for other river animals. That ensures there is plenty of wildlife living in the river, including insect larvae, the following spring. At that time a new generation of alevins emerges from the gravel and grows into fry. The salmon's cycle of life is ready to start all over again.

Words to Know

Alevin A newly hatched salmon with its yolk sac attached.

Biologists Scientists who study living things.

Fertilized When a sperm and egg come together to make a new individual.

Fins Parts of its body that a fish uses to balance, propel, and steer itself.

Freshwater Water that is not salty. Rivers and lakes contain freshwater.

Fry A young salmon after it has used up its yolk sac and started to feed itself. Salmon fry are also called parr.

Gills Feathery structures in a fish's head that take in oxygen from water.

Krill	Tiny, pink, shrimplike, sea creatures that are an adult salmon's main food.
Larvae	The early stage of an insect's life after it hatches from an egg. Many insect larvae live in water.
Predators	Animals that hunt other animals.
Prey	An animal that is hunted for food.
Smolt	A young salmon that is large enough to make the journey to the ocean.
Redd	A fish's nest made by hollowing out the gravel at the bottom of the water.
Spawn	A way of breeding in which a female lays her eggs and leaves before the male's sperm fertilizes the eggs.
Sperm	A substance produced by males to fertilize eggs.

Find Out More

Books

Goldish, M. *Salmon and Other Bony Fish*. Chicago, Illinois: World Book, 2002.

Martin-James, K. *Swimming Salmon*. Minneapolis, Minnesota: Lerner Publications Co., 2003.

Trumbauer, Lisa. *The Life Cycle of a Salmon*. Mankato, Minnesota: Pebble Books, 2003.

Web sites

Salmon Life Cycle Quiz
www.enchantedlearning.com/subjects/fish/printouts/Salmon.shtml
A life-cycle printout and quiz.

SalmonCam
wdfw.wa.gov/wildwatch/salmoncam/index.html
A webcam showing activity at a salmon farm.

Index